W9-CKT-367

PERENNIAL FALL

PHOENIX **POETS**

❧ *Perennial Fall* ☙

MAGGIE DIETZ

THE UNIVERSITY OF CHICAGO PRESS
Chicago and London

MAGGIE DIETZ is lecturer in creative writing at Boston University and assistant poetry editor for *Slate* magazine. She is the coeditor most recently of *An Invitation to Poetry: A New Favorite Poem Project Anthology* (2004).

The University of Chicago Press, Chicago 60637
The University of Chicago Press, Ltd., London
© 2006 by The University of Chicago
All rights reserved. Published 2006
Printed in the United States of America

15 14 13 12 11 10 09 08 07 06   1 2 3 4 5

ISBN: 0-226-14849-1   (cloth)
ISBN: 0-226-14850-5   (paper)

Library of Congress Cataloging-in-Publication Data

Dietz, Maggie.
    Perennial fall / Maggie Dietz.
      p. cm. — (Phoenix poets)
    ISBN 0-226-14849-1 (cloth : alk. paper) — ISBN 0-226-14850-5 (pbk. : alk. paper)
    I. Title. II. Series.

    PS3604.I375P47 2006
    811'.6—dc22

                                                            2005017093

♾ The paper used in this publication meets the minimum requirements of the American National Standard for Information Sciences—Permanence of Paper for Printed Library Materials, ANSI Z39.48-1992.

for T

Contents

Acknowledgments

Grateful acknowledgment is made to the editors of the publications in which the following poems first appeared, some as earlier versions:

AGNI: "The Yellow House, 1978," "Altos II" appeared as
     "Altos de Chavon (I)"
Beloit Poetry Journal: "Speaking for Andrew"
The Boston Globe: "Collector"
Bostonia: "What's Become" appeared as "What's Become: A Love Note"
The Carolina Quarterly: "Hinge"
Grolier Poetry Prize Annual (1999): "When She Asked I Said No You Cannot
     Play with It"
Harvard Review: "The Interview"
Literary Imagination: "Matthew 6: 19–21"
Memorious: "Why I Don't Piss in the Ocean," "Altos III"
Poetry: "Paisano" appeared as "Paisano (and What Flashes in the Sky)"
Provincetown Arts: "Altos I" appeared as "Altos de Chavon (II)"
Salmagundi: "Perpetual Between," "Bright Lament," "Cotton Anniversary"
Seattle Review: "Circle of Horses"
Shankpainter: "Bath"
Slate: "Seasonal"

"The Yellow House, 1978" appeared on Poetry Daily and was reprinted in *AGNI* 56, the Thirtieth Anniversary Poetry Anthology.

I finished many of these poems while I was writer-in-residence at Phillips Exeter Academy, and during a winter fellowship at the Fine Arts Work Center in Provincetown. To those places, and the friends and colleagues I found there, abundant thanks.

I am grateful to my teachers: RuthAnn Reynen, Father Gordon Gilsdorf, Joanna Anos, Anne Winters, David Ferry, Aaron Fogel, Rosanna Warren, and Robert Pinsky; and to my readers: Jill McDonough, Nicole Long, Ilya Kaminsky, and my husband, Todd Hearon.

Infinite thanks to my family—especially to my parents, Richard and Candace Dietz.

I

Three Dog Night

I
I held the retriever in the dream
like a bouquet of lilies, the yellow
weight of her will-less. In my pocket,
a flap of ear—another loved dog's—
a broken-off paw. "See," I told the man
at the scale, "it's been very hard."
I argued that the dogs once weighed
more than the parts I'd managed to keep.
"Not enough," he said, as the sun began
to rise. "You see your girl is coming
back to life," and sure enough, the dog
fell from the counter flopping like a fish,
unfolding, glowing. "I have suffered,"
I said, hushing the dog who was now
standing upright, holding my hand.
"Not enough," he said. "Your other dead?"
"I have photos," I told him. "You will
have more." "Dogs?" I asked him.
"Dogs just get you in the door."

II

In the cage: a guinea pig, a hamster.
At the bottom a small mole, soft
and cold. Later I hear the stirring,
pretend to sleep through the birth.
(In the first grade . . . Maureen
McCarthy, her gerbils' pink
babies, her sisters' extravagant
earring trees shaped like ladders.)
Something good is happening
in the dark. When I open it,
the cage is filled with hay and
lying there is a tiny jaguar ·
with round ears, a rounded face
and elaborate black patterns in
his deliriously soft fur. Warm
weight. Small beauty. I am happy
but will need a bigger house.

III

I'm walking down Lakeshore Drive
in Milwaukee and a complicated form
descends. You are there, changing
identities. "A bird!" you say. "An eagle!"
It carries some struggling prey
that tumbles from its clutch in front
of us. A haggard terrier, with dark eyes
like my nephew's. I lift it up; it nuzzles
my elbow, coughs. The cartoonish bird,
its eyes like plates, is angry, pacing
about like an eighteenth-century gentleman
with brown knickers, yellow tights.
He charges, undeterred by my humanity,
tries to snap at the dog in my arms,
who yelps and squirms. Then he drives
his beak into my leg—hard—my arm.
Burning with pain, I kick his face. You
don't know what to do or have gone
away. I run to the couple leaving
their car. "The dog," I shout, and they
let me shove him inside, then lock
the doors and leave. No eagle
in sight. You take my hand. But wait—
I want the little dog! No, that's not it.
I want to be thanked for saving him.

North of Boston

Hoarfrost coats and cuffs
the playing fields, a heyday
of glistening. So there's hope
in my throat as I walk across them
to the woods with my chest
flung open, spilling its coins.
The light so bright I can hear it,
a silver tone like a penny whistle.

It's fall, so I'm craving pine cones.
Hundreds of maples the color
of bulldozers!

       But something strange
is going on: the trees are tired
of meaning, sick of providing
mystery, parallels, consolation.
"Leave us alone," they seem to cry,
with barely energy for a pun.

The muscular river crawls on
its belly in a maple coat of mail.
Muddy and unreflective, it smells
as if it too could use some privacy.

The sumac reddens like a face,
holding out its velvet pods
almost desperately. The Queen
Anne's Lace clicks in the wind.

A deaf-mute milkweed
foaming at the mouth.

Back at the field I look
for what I didn't mean
to drop. The grass is green.

        Okay, Day,
my host, I want to get out
of your house. Come on, Night,
with your twinkly stars and big
dumb moon. Tell me don't
show me, and wipe that grin
off your face.

When She Asked I Said No You Cannot Play with It

I really don't mind but that the dolls are so fragile—
wire and fabric with plastic heads, hands and shoes.
My favorite the one with the dull yellow braids,

a present from my godmother who last month
had a breast removed and the same breast built again.
The doll wore a red skirt, which I long ago lost,

but her bloomers can pass as shorts. When her legs
unraveled she sat in my father's dresser with his change
and his comb and the bills for months until, finally,

one Saturday, I begged him to fix her and he sutured
the felt-skin to the doll's bones, cinched it into her shoes
with a manicure tool and some superglue.

Our neighbor, Mr. VandeLoo, built the house for me.
There are only two like it—the other his granddaughter's.
He's dead now. We paid him forty dollars.

It was made of plain wood so I elaborated, labored
for hours, gluing the wooden siding lip over ridge and affixing
hundreds of cracker-sized cedar shingles to the roof.

I peeled bit prints out of wallpaper books and used
the pinking shears to make curtains, hung on toothpicks,
for the windows my father cut from the walls with a jigsaw.

On Easter Sunday my niece was pleased by our similar
dresses, hers pink and mine blue, both long and flowered.
And I took her to the park though I was buckled with cramps

and gave her chocolate before dinner. But when she asked
about the house I told her softly no, and no I said
to the thumb-sized toilet and frosted sink, the pewter

apples and silverware, the wooden plates,
the blank-paged books, the brass roses
greening on the mantle over an endless fire.

No to the gingham bunkbeds, to the false-doored china hutch
and no to the yellow-haired delicate doll, though I know
she would gladly be broken again to be touched.

Cotton Anniversary

Then after four moves and a hundred Tuesdays
I was alone in a house you hadn't seen in a town
surrounded by water, wearing a dead woman's rings.

It was October again. We'd been through thirteen
rainstorms, two fierce winters, a burial and forty
hangovers. Your good old dog died that first winter

and was burned. I could not remember my dreams,
not one. It was as if I never had them. The colors
changed, and the traffic. The illusion of season

tricked me into late sleep, squash soup, sweaters.
No matter what, the tides came in like the packages
of used books I ordered from the Internet.

The days hid behind the nights, and ten, twenty
of them skulked by. A thing about the past:
it gets longer, but it never leaves. The seventy-

sextillion stars remain affixed to certain space.
What I had: one cotton T-shirt you had worn
and left the relic of your scent upon. I slept

with it covering my face until my sweat and spittle
steeped the cloth, the trace of you cast out
like ash or unremembered dreams or days.

Why I Don't Piss in the Ocean

Once my sister told me that from her summit at the city
pool she could see the yellow billows spread like gas
or dreams between kids' legs. In something the size of the sea,
you can't be sure who's watching from above. Let's say
it's the Almighty, twirling His whistle, ready to blow it
at any moment and let loose the bottomless Apocalypse:
the ocean would make bone of a body, coral of bone.
Piss, and a tiger-fish darts through a skull-hole, a weed
weaves itself through ribs. You, too, have seen
the bulbs flash from the sea. You, too, have felt
it breathing down your neck. You eat fish. You've heard
that mermaids sing. My dreams are as beleaguered as the next
Joe's, my happiness as absurd, but I'm not going to go
piss in the ocean about it. No, not in the ocean.

Circle of Horses

Dingy, rough-hided, they were ridden down,
round the ring and round the mound,
the ponies with giant hooves and faces.

The blue-veined tips of their ears twitching,
they rocked onward never swifter though
the riders hollered "giddy'up" and "ya"
and kicked imaginary spurs into their ribs.

Tethered as to a maypole, they wore
the earth empty, left not a comet-trail
but a crater from a donut-shaped meteor:
the ground untrodden risen in the middle—
a burial mound, or the conquering hump
of the funhouse Sugar-Bowl carved of oak.

They were old, but almost foals.
On Sisyphus, On Virgil. Laborers and
guides: digging, showing the way down.

In Dante's hell they'd dwell with
the poets just across the river:
the Ancients, the Unbaptized.

Blanketed in the stables, they slept
the sleep of the dead. They rested.

They didn't dream of Shetland Isles
or the blue-green view from Assateague.

Bright Lament

Here where the sun washes
The old furniture white and gold,
Where petals crepe and sink like eyelids,
And in the corner the copper bowl
Is decorative that once was used
By able hands in making bread
And sweets; here in the half-life
Of morning, I read that death
Undid another come undone,
A girl who in the note she left said
I am already tired. Already tired
And twelve years old and gone.

What's here? Some things we think
We earned and some things left us,
The light that's given whether
Or not we want it, whether or not
It's appropriate, and touches things
That do not ask to gleam. No thing
Can hold a human hurt, the heart
Endures or doesn't. One wants
To offer something, but is tired.
In another room, thank God,
Good shades, and the rumpled bed
Still open, still unmade.

Paisano

The clouds still differentiate the dark.
At nearly midnight, light they incubate
makes silver nightshade bloom between the stars.

The day I saw a jackrabbit is ending
for its only time, so I know more than when
these clouds were born a blown time ago.

Midnight: the porch hovers and we lean
in chairs, with glistening bottles, move our arms,
our mouths (but not to kiss, and not to speak).

The dog boxes a June bug with his shadow
like a fox. It's Texas—now and then a star
will blaze a trail past here to where it goes,

a bird will summon Chuck Will's widow
though she'll never come, as I have called a ghost
who's lost, who's lost someone. There is no room

for that old desolation here. The house
is small, the pasture rough with things to find.
The night is kindly lit, and you are kind.

And what will happen is another day.
The rain-lily will spring beneath the wheel.
The flycatcher will poke its crested head

out of the martin house. I know these names,
and saw a scarlet wasp above the prickly pear.
I saw the place the star made when it fell.

I saw you say I love you to the dark,
and watched a fast shape dive into the light
of the rabbit-hole in Mexico, the moon.

II

Perpetual Between

A book a hinge, the page a hinge.

The mind, this way and that, a hinge.

Your hand, opening the music of

the instrument, a hinge. The instrument

a hinge. The mood hinged upon

the song. The song a hinge. And you

and I—o metaphysicians—hinges.

The body hinged: the jaw, the lids,

the valves. The house a hinge, holding

things in and out. The moment opens,

closes, opens, closes. The night. The clock.

The thought. The heart. The door. The breath.

Back Yard with Figures

In light the color of sand, of the hides
of deer, a child bent over a cricket,

the shape of the bent child a cricket.
The cricket and a woman sang.

It was from another time, the song
that found her throat as she pinned white

sheets to the line beside the house.
It was as if the line had brought the song.

She pinned and lifted, feeling
again the rhythms of the once-

loved, how they'd so often moved.
The song or the wind brought salt

to her eyes. The sheets were sails,
the curtains at the window ghosts

as a warm salt draught curled
out from the kitchen. Moving

to the woman's song, the boy
sailed, a bug between the sheets.

They stayed awhile in the old song,
the tired light, the smell of supper,

as the cricket's singing drew its lines
around them and between them.

Altos I

Nothing dampened their cries, not
the plush air nor the brush under the palms.

The mango trees swelled like the mother
cat's belly, which by mutation had
no nipples but had filled with milk.

The kittens tore at the bulges until she bled.
We separated them, fed the kittens bread
soaked in water we'd boiled on the stove.

One of five would survive, and the mother
whose milk dried up like the parched arroyos.
We kept her cool with damp towels.

The shopkeeper's daughter would keep them
against her father's wishes, and the name—
Chispita—we gave the blue-eyed kitten.

The guard saw everything and asked
if we wanted mangoes, angling for a tip.

What were these if not apparitions?
Slight girl carrying a pitcher, grown
man climbing a tree. The moon

looked cool but gave no relief from
the heat that climbed our limbs, the new
need nothing we knew would reach.

The Interview

It was like living again.

When he retired from the sea, the old man
built ships in bottles with needlefish-like instruments.
He worked the keel from a log's natural arch, whittled bowsprits
and sanded them smooth. His pince-nez resting low, he'd bow
to look into the world which bit by painstaking bit he built.

The child came often to watch,
but could not touch the sails like moth wings,
the copper-knobbed topgallant mast
(from pennies melted in a crucible).

The ships were frail, the bottles seaworthy—
corked and sealed with wax.

The old man never looked up.
"What's it like to be old?" asked the child.
"It's like being young. You have terrible secrets."

The crow's nest needs a lookout man,
he thought, *the deck a cannon.*

Only the child and the man
would know the clipper hull
was lined with mother-of-pearl.

One day the old man gave
the child a bottle painted black.
"Is there a ship inside?" asked the child.

The old man went on looking in, not up.

The child took his prize to the piers.

Wood Bowl

Old purpose,
some hands turned you
with old skill

Mouth for oranges,
onions or warm
bread—Open:

Echo dome,
breast, lens and
half-world

Outlast us,
object, hold
another's fruit—

The possibility of being
filled of being
overturned
of floating

Round, old tool:
moon belly skiff
bowl skull

Elegy

Today I heard from him that lives
there now that you are dead.

When you were ours, your eye wept
and head swung lower than the others'.

The buzzards led him to the creek bed
and there you were pecked open, pink with
your spotted hide peeled back and eyeless.

The two longhorns still left
roam the acres together eating
nettles as if nothing happened.

They'll have their turns.
The brindled one was getting thin.

This new guy says he'll bury your skull
with salt and resurrect it on the wall.

So I may see you yet.

The Yellow House, 1978

The kitchen in the house had a nook for eating, a groove
for the broom behind the door and the woman moved through
it like bathing, reaching ladles from drawers, turning to lift

the milk from the refrigerator while still stirring the pudding,
as if the room and everything in it were as intimate to her as her
body, as beautiful and worthy of her attention as the elbows

which each day she soothed with rose lotion or the white legs
she lifted, again and again, in turn, while watching television.
To be in that room must be what it was like to be the man

next to her at night, or the child who, at six o'clock had stood
close enough to smell the wool of her sweater through the steam,
and later, at the goodnight kiss, could breathe the flavor of her hair—

codfish and broccoli—and taste the coffee, which was darkness
on her lips, and listen then from upstairs to the water running
down, the mattress drifting down the river, a pale moonmark

on the floor, and hear the clink of silverware—the stars, their distant
speaking—and picture the ceiling—the back of a woman kneeling,
covering the heart and holding up the bed and roof and cooling sky.

Altos II

Light crested as the leaves moved from
green to green, like breathing.

From the roof: jungle, cane and sea
moved to the rhythms of wind, sickle
and tide—various bodies,

none more naked than the pink,
transparent lizards whose entire workings—
gut, muscle and vein—were visible to
the naked eye as they climbed the walls
visible through them.

Evenings, music and the hard-
working moon—so many chinks and spaces
through which to make patterns.

Bodies moved together in patterns
toward nakedness.

Beneath us, the cats brawled, fucked,
and cried like babies, cried so high and deep
the music couldn't drown them out.

Now and then, a mango fell with a thud
or a giant moth made shapes against the flames.

Among the welcome elements not one
thing did not hunger to be changed.
The heat held still between us.

Bird Bath

How could it have been otherwise
the year he died? The ice hastened
its surprise, one day descended.

Apples froze in clusters on
the branches, glass apples on glass trees.
Any false move would end them.

Our mother's heart fell down around
her knees, knocked between her ankles,
tripping her up. We held her

like a doll, a rag doll—her eyes
glass buttons, shining but not seeing.
Mute eyes dreaming a sense

of heaven, of what is next. But
everywhere the bald world and cold.
The snow, the clouds, the frozen ground.

Our fatherless mother not like our
mother, the one with the father.
From the piano, chords of her anger

roamed the house. Tears fell from her
clean, wet hair. The coffee grinder
screamed, and went silent.

The day she laughed ice cracked
the bird bath. Its halves lay in the snow.
One was the past, and one the future.

Collector

The Chinese master of balance rides his balance-machine
each morning along Jamaica Pond. The morning

traffic can witness his trembling determination
as he moves toward the center for redemption,

where he trades the contents of his magnificent balloons
for food, rent and equipment: rolls of twine, blue

translucent bags, and cotton gardening gloves
if they come cheap. His hands must dive

all night in and out of trash barrels, like seals
after glistening fish. He needs the moon, unfolds

and fills bag after bag, the plastic bottles not thrown,
but wound neatly into spiral rows like bales then

tied in the particular order of balance to the bicycle,
first to the back fender, then to the seat, falling left, until

by 7:00 a.m. the bicycle is invisible beneath the layers
of gigantic bags, piled taller than the man and broader

than the path along the pond, which he has reached,
now close to rest. He launches there at the eastern edge,

tilting the bicycle up that had leaned against him as he went,
then down to mount, the right foot on its pedal, the left

slowly revving along the walk. Like a child first learning
to ride, he wobbles as he begins, his legs bowed out, leaning

too far right, then, the handlebars violently wobbling,
gripping tight, knees straightening, body striving

forward instead of side to side. He challenges the air,
steering the vessel, letting the wind in his hair

tell him which way to pull and where to put his weight.
On blustery days, it seems he might take flight,

the bags puffing like massive lungs. When he brings
them out of the center, they are skins, stretched and flimsy.

He folds them on the ground, one by one, corner
to corner, then ties the weightless bundle to the fender.

Then he goes, also empty, loosening his sleeves,
riding to ride, easy and ready for sleep.

Altos III

The sun hauled its cart across the sky—
not a god, a god's weary ox. Summer
had begun to hurt, and the forbidden river
was too much for us, so we went to it.
The great stone stairway seemed to call
with its lost grandeur for our hands and feet,
echo of the commerce it sustained when it
sustained the place. We had no history for it—
the stones each three feet deep and six
feet wide, each perhaps a ton and like a tomb.
We started down them—scrambling with our hands,
sitting to jump where one had crumbled clean
away, our palms and bottoms chalk-white when
three-hundred slabs later we reached the slow water.
Our faces glistened like coins. A man approached
in a wooden boat, as if he had expected us;
a small man, with a face like dried fruit.
He offered us a ride. At the prow,
a basket of slim silver fish, still breathing;
a sack of mangoes hard as yellow stones.
The man pulled the boat, low with our
weight, downriver with one warped oar.
One of us laughed at the wretched cows
that called and grazed on the far, flat bank,
their hides hanging from their spines like rags.
A boy, the cowherd, slept against a tree.

Then we were quiet. Green became green.
Nothing flickered. The light found all things
equally until we slowed under a grotto of leaves.
A bright green and turquoise bird cried
across the water, blurring its wings.
As if it were a sign, the old man stirred
the boat around, and then he sang.
The voice stirred like the wings of birds,
flocked with startling color from his throat—
it rose and deepened, now thin, now clear,
a woman's voice, a boy's. I couldn't
get all the words: *arboles . . . ojos . . .*
corazón . . . lejos. The music scaled
the cliff, then fell again like leaves onto
the water. He held a brittle note, then stopped
and dropped us at the riverbank. We paid
him for a photo, slung our arms around
his shoulders. There were the stairs in front
of us like years. We paid him for the ride.

Hinge

In a damp camel wool coat
      The door-hinges creaked
Thickened with Winston smoke
      Fresh snow on the fedora's rim
He waited for them
      Turning to dew in the kitchen
Until they came from their work
      Steam rising from his shoulders
Assembling oranges and cloves
      Like smoke
Losing the oranges, rusted as hinges
      His eyes invisible
(Like bushes surrounded with bees)
      Behind glasses frosted as flutes
They flocked to that place
      In the safe cupboard
Where sturdy arms lifted them up
      Where they waited
Their hands coated in cloves
      For champagne
In the damp steam and smoke
      For something to celebrate
Hanging like ornaments from him
      His cheeks cold as bottles
In the palimpsest of nightfall
      Brought up from the basement

The day's early troubles
    That dampened the focus
Dissolved in the nearness of task
    Of hunger, even of pleasure
And the clock's round distance
    Which also wanted rest
From the next to next

Bath

for Jill

Here is the porcelain tub: expectant, cool,
its ledges lined with lavender and lemon,
labeled jars of mud and salt and oil,
milled soaps that smell of rose or melon,

oatmeal scrub and peppermint shampoo,
black wedge of pumice, ocean sponge, a bristled
brush with oaken handle—all for you,
who love abundance of particulars.

Now turn the H and let the rising vapor
cloud the aging tiles and oval mirror.
Make tea or a martini, grab the paper
or a yellowed novel. Tie your tumbling hair,

and watch as the tipped liquid turns to lace:
Here are your waters and your watering place.

Colleen in Sonoma

Fragments from the unsent letters

*

Mornings I wake and wash my face in the enamel basin,
look into the mirror hung on the balsam.

My place is here. The sun blooms clean. My face
framed bare against the ancient mountains.

*

My son sleeps. He wakes.

His tears fall like leaves, his laughter falls—
drops of water onto water.

So my lover's not my child's father.
I love his thistle beard, his orange heart.

*

We left Green Bay, the family house, at dusk.
The paper plants along the river churned,
waved papery flags of coal-smoke at the sun.
The river dragged its heels beneath the busted
railroad bridge. (That bridge—a giant cricket
with feet on either bank. The trains once made
it sing, and its dark iron shone like shell.)

The strip malls glowed fluorescent as TVs.
A flag waved over gravestones. The sky blazed.
Gulls in the distance spelled words with their wings.

*

We slept at the shore of the sky, the stars
flecks of sun on the tips of the sea.

Blue light swept through the trees
in waves, swept through me like water.

I wanted to be still, to be moved.

*

States rose and fell and rose in front of us.
Gas stations surfaced like electric islands.
The wires along the highway peaked and dove.
Quinn slept and woke as we drove West and West.
The dream we kept awake was *California*:
mountains that crest and dive into blue valleys;
the ocean an island—sturdy, permanent;
vineyards glistening green and gray and green.

*

Like sardines, they say, in our broken
bug-green camper and *that's no way
to raise a child*. The pay phone hums.

The stars over that fenced yard were
often asterisks, marking exceptions.

*

After rain, arms of light
fold shade like sheets.

Underneath: coniferous
green and mineral hardness.

The immutable speaks.
Anyone can hear who listens.

The ocean's seven miles off.
I taste its vapor in my throat.

*

Wind today, and the sheets tussle
with the clothespins. I moved
here. I came here to live.

Milwaukee, distant—the drugged,
enduring dream from which
I woke up pregnant.

Marriage then, boiling water
to bathe the infant in the cold
unrenovated cheese factory
with cheap rent in the country.

Cow shit on our shoes. I woke
to a hell of ghosts and called you,
grit in the windows, no help,

I hated, had to, packed the baby
and drove straight to you told me so.

*

Quinn is warm and cool.
My face blooms in his dream
then in his eyes, my voice
in his ears. He raises his arms:
I lift the damp shirt over
his head, wash him with
a cloth, with cool water.

*

Our days are blue and green and brown.
My child rides a swing between the trees.
The mountains rise and fall. The birds fly
to and fro—the blue, green and brown birds.

*

Home was coal, was corn . . .
You know those faces
bald as bowls. And
cold for months. Don't
get me wrong: I know
the kind of care it took
to get me here . . .
and love: hearts broad
as the Wisconsin vowels.

*

Shut your worries. For years
I prayed someone would show
me how to live and someone did.
If you come, I'll show you:

Pacific dusk, the coastal shoals
of weary seals huddled on sand.
The sun bold at the end of sight.

At night, the stars are like—
sardines, white-silver, tight as fists.

III

Matthew 6: 19–21

Hold off awhile, moth and
rust and thieves—for I love

this world, my heart is
here, where a body breathes.

I've seen such treasures, even
of your making: night's wool,

the frayed holes light comes
through. Burnt sky cracking

the corroded ocean Octobers
the sun goes. Thieves have

taken grief, and the thing
one hated most. So keep

your work up elsewhere, leave
me my store. The young

geologist radioed *THIS IS
IT* before St. Helens sank

him, seized in a dream:
treasure of rupture and force.

What does one fear if not a
loss? How do days in the next

world pass? Nothing to tend,
nothing you're up against.

No moth, no rust. O Lord let
there be thieves among the angels.

Wisconsin, Insomnia

Outside our sleep, third shift. The mills along
the river lit and burning.
                        Skin of sleep,
thin as the antique mirror's speckling silver
or the sheen upon a river halved by light.
Stirrup, cochlea, a low vibration floating
through the fan: pipe organ at the hollow Abbey—
a hum in the teeth before each mournful chord
breaks against marble, banks in flesh and wood.
Again.
        Just the late freighter steaming out
its only speech—exhausted, clockwork call.
Decades since my brother bent the shade
to watch the blistered coal cars sliding past
like boats.
            Boatless river, birdless at this hour.
Had Hades waited there'd have been a train
along the Styx. The Fox shudders when the train
groans by. I've seen its surface break to bits
beneath the burden of that sound, and re-
assemble.
          The rosary on the mirror clicks,
saying itself—or is it the woman whose face
aged there? Ancestral novena—bless her,
pray for us sinners.
                    There's comfort in superstition,

and in the steady engine of the fan.
The mirror trembles, the tarnished water, unseen
pictures rippling. It keeps us in the dark.
Tonight I'd give up all my sleep to glimpse
Which one of us will be the first to board
That train and where and if we'll be delivered.

The furniture, the room, is as it was.
When did this body grow into this bed?
Now the young are old; the old are dead.
What comfort?
               Electric breeze, worn eyelet sheets,
Your body's rhythmic industry, its warmth.
As it is, ever shall be. Again, the whistle—
This is where I'm from.
                   Day and night
Fresh fuel arrives and fresh men load the fires.
The stacks perpetual snuffed-out candles smoldering
Thin, continuous clouds above the town.
Late summer the water boils with silver carp.
A mile from here bent willows knit their roots
Into the river's edge. And there below the bridge:
The dam's endless falls, the fugitive pelicans.

Neighborhood

What I had wanted is gone and whom
I loved, and the songs we sang after supper.

The stairs still creak under me, and
the leaves lift their beaks to the sun.

Children throw sticks in the mud;
their mothers pack tidy lunches.

The clouds, not shaped like anything,
pretend to be; so the game continues.

A stock-boy shelves tomatoes.
The Florida strawberries have arrived.

The wind plays its instruments: I am one,
and the multicolored clothing on the wire.

The sycamore has changed its clothes again;
the woman across the street, her hair.

At night the windows flash out purple codes,
and shapes of people move from room to room.

The streetlights and insects buzz and hum.
In one house of many stories a light burns.

What's Become

In your absence the trees are thick with sap,
catching slugs, amber jewels for our inheritors.
The cones so thin and weak I can eat them.

Everything is strange. Where the sky once met
the garden there's a wool of yellow smoke.
The sparrow I threw into it did not come back.

The dog will not follow me anymore.
The squirrels hang like fish over the branches
and the birds tunnel deeper into the earth.

In the kitchen: the skull of an orange,
some mites that might have been seeds;
the potatoes, damp mouths, gone to talking.

There is a chalk horse standing in the briar.
Every time he moves he is eliminated.
His ghosts go one by one into the woods.

Even now, I look for you in every direction,
though my eyes are opals, my hands rope.
I write you: hieroglyphs, shaken from the stem.

If you know I am waiting, please come.
It's been too long since the brick house
with its fence and grass and marigolds.

Seasonal

Summer-long the gulls' old umbra cry
unraveled ease
but certain waves went by, then by.
The sky shook out the days.

The seabirds' hunger rose in rings,
flung rock-clams to their shatterings,
raked gullets full, the bone-bills scraped.

High noon: oceans of time escaped.

                    *

All winter we slept benched together,
breakers, sleepdrunk children in a car
not conscious where they go.

We kneaded bread, kept out the weather,
while old suspicions huddled by the door,
mice in the snow.

                    *

In spring, the leaving bloomed—
oak leaf unfurled, a foot, resplendent

vigorous, aching to shake loose
but still dependent.

One morning moongreen loaves
rose into bones that rose to lift
our skin like sleeves,
our time together's revenant.

*

Perennial fall, come cool the cliffs,
bring quiet, sulfur, early dark.
Represent as you must: dusk, dying, ends
and row us into winter's water:

The body, wind-whipped, forms stiff peaks,
ice settles in the marrow bone.
At the chest, the live stone breaks against the beak,
beak breaks against stone.

Prayer to a Suicide

Brother when they laid you down
I touched the break in lashes
where the chicken pox had blown

the lid up long ago, small brushes
that stroked out your seeing hours.
I wish the clouds would wash us

down with unrepentant power,
that pounding rain would soak in
to your newly opened grave. Our

mother's breath is broken,
her C scar tingles after many years.
Our father has not spoken.

All night the faucet drives hard tears
down into the silent house.
They say it is beyond repair.

Wherever you are, cry for us.

Speaking for Andrew

In Memoriam A. G., 1973–1999

In the woods I found the mouth that made the voice—

calling back all the way, some six hundred days,
to Vancouver, where I'd parked my Jeep and realized
I had no plan, but friends already in Portland,
a screened-in porch and good zoning laws that gave
everyone a vista of the mountains. I hadn't seen them yet
or coursed their veins:

> *O beautiful land where the mouth*
> *that housed that voice bent down, engulfed me.*

So then I had it: informant, teller, the big old talker.
I had it and I went to work landscaping. Dug it.
One night I walked away from the table where we were eating,
yucking it up, bought a beer at the bar, poured it,
didn't drink it, walked out onto the gray street
and up and up into the trails and off the trails.
Next morning, I found my car in the driveway. I took
a few things and drove to L.A. without stopping.

The way I told it later I lost my wallet and my mind
on the same day. That was when I could still joke about it,
before the voice took up with crows and fenceposts,
before it found my own throat and spoke through me.
In the city of angels I heard a number, dialed it—

How many days then on the street?—I heard a voice,
clear and open, one that had reached me long ago
through another cord: the voice of an angel. I said,
"I think I'm your son."

                     In North Carolina, they set me up
with a good shrink and some numbing drugs, good ones.
My mother made hearty meals for me, smoothed my hair
when she passed me watching TV. After a while I got a job
at a bakery, got baked a lot with the Mexican guys
who worked in the garden. I started planting trees again.
I wrote to my friends and got my own apartment,
where the voice didn't seem to find me even in dreams.

                         * *

Around Thanksgiving I buckled, but not weakly—
tenderly, as if someone had kissed my ear. I surrendered.
Some front from a northern wind blew you back
down to me, from Vancouver, from the greater North,
further, from the oldest pilgrimage, the other side
of sky, you the voice of millions, like echoes from
the recess of a cave, compounded, fragmented,
sacred and sacrilege, speaking in tongues. I heard you,
everywhere, I joined you. And no one understood,
could see how big it all was how old how deep.

* * *

One night, in the snare of my vision I caught a dark man
with joints of light brandishing the moon like a hatchet.
Great Orion, wounding the sky, make a clean hack for me.
And I thought the sky was black liquid, the stars
silver fish and shells.

        I left my car in the woods,
not hidden, a good car, a good find, and found my way,
now farther South, to the water, using a broken stick
and the daylit image of my starborn father. The birds
were singing alleluias and the canopy illumined
like a halo in the hollowed woods. It was not a dark day,
it was not. Even when night came the oily thick
dark glistened.

When my guide arrived he shone on the pond,
shimmering from the belt and elbows. Now the frogs
spoke of origin, material, the mud we come from.
I threw a stone to provoke him and, seeing my signal,
he moved. The moon, a perfect scythe, flinched in his arm.
My opening. And through it rang a chorus of every voice
that ever was. I heard them each and all and in that moment
knew, for just a moment, what it means to love and suffer,
please believe me, what it is to die and live.